The Brontës
& Haworth

PAUL WHITE

Whinray Books · Ilkley

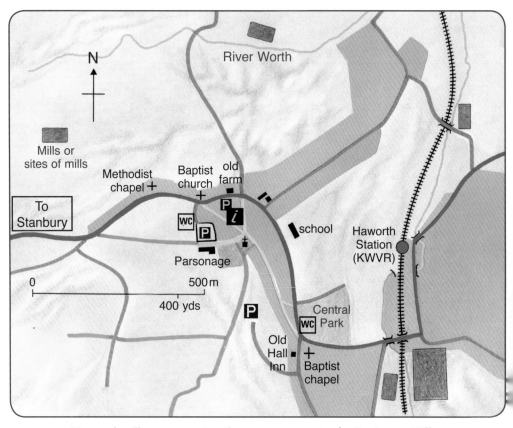

Haworth village centre. See the map on page 38 for Penistone Hill, Stanbury, Ponden and Top Withens

First published 2012 by Whinray Books, an imprint of
Bossiney Books Ltd, 33 Queens Drive, Ilkley, West Yorkshire LS29 9QW

© 2012 Paul White

ISBN 978-0-9571939-0-1

Acknowledgements
The portraits on pages 5 and 7 are reproduced by
kind permission of the Brontë Parsonage Museum.
The maps are by Graham Hallowell, photographs by the author.

Printed in Great Britain by R Booth Limited, Penryn, Cornwall

Introduction

Jane Eyre, apparently written by 'Currer Bell', burst upon the London literary scene in October 1847. Everyone was soon asking, who is this newcomer whose passionate writing is so unlike that of any of the established authors?

By December, the book was a runaway best-seller, and received rave reviews: 'decidedly the best book of the season', 'a book of decided power', 'all serious novel writers of the day lose in comparison with Currer Bell'.

Then a different publisher launched two further novels: *Wuthering Heights* by Ellis Bell, and *Agnes Grey* by Acton Bell, and this intrigued the London literary world even more.

How were the three authors related? Were they men or women? They seemed to know how women thought and felt, yet they showed 'the brutalising influence of unchecked passion' and far too much knowledge of debauchery and wickedness for them to be 'ladies'. Some pundits thought all three books were by one author.

In those days new novels were hugely expensive – a guinea and a half, the equivalent of a month's wages for a labourer. Succcessful books came out in cheaper editions later, but most readers used 'circulating libraries' which were rather like today's public libraries, except funded by individual subscriptions rather than from taxation. Before long, *Jane Eyre* in particular was being read throughout the country, including Yorkshire.

But the year 1848 brought a change. Reviewers began to attack all three writers as being obsessed with unpleasant and offensive subject matter. This culminated in an extraordinary review in *The Quarterly*. Here is a sample:

> Altogether the autobiography of *Jane Eyre* is pre-eminently
> an anti-Christian composition. There is throughout it a
> murmuring against the comforts of the rich and against
> the privations of the poor, which, as far as each individual is
> concerned, is a murmuring against God's appointment – there
> is a proud and perpetual assertion of the rights of man, for
> which we find no authority either in God's word or in God's
> providence – there is that pervading tone of ungodly
> discontent which is at once the most prominent and the most

subtle evil which the law and the pulpit, which all civilised society in fact has at the present day to contend with. We do not hesitate to say that the tone of mind and thought which has overthrown authority and violated every code human and divine abroad, and fostered Chartism and rebellion at home, is the same which has also written *Jane Eyre*.

1848 was 'the year of Revolutions' in Europe, and there was a fear among the ruling classes (an entirely justified fear) that Britain too would succumb to revolution – or mob rule, as they saw it. There were cracks in the Establishment, but for aristocratic Tories the Chartist demand that all men should have the vote was a threat to Godliness.

It was in 1848 that Mrs Cecil Frances Alexander wrote the children's hymn 'All things bright and beautiful', still sung today, but usually with the following verse omitted:

> The rich man in his castle,
> The poor man at his gate,
> God made them high and lowly,
> And ordered their estate.

It is of course easier to accept this view if God has ordered you a 20,000 acre estate than if you have to watch your parents, after a lifetime of labour, thrust into the workhouse, separated and starved. And there was plenty of that kind of injustice visible in the Brontës' Haworth.

Three further novels by 'the Bell brothers' followed, *The Tenant of Wildfell Hall* (1848) by Acton Bell, and *Shirley* (1849) and *Villette* (1853) from Currer.

The truth about their authorship came out only in 1850, after the deaths of 'Ellis' (Emily) and 'Acton' (Anne): it was Emily and Anne who had demanded anonymity. Suddenly Charlotte Brontë was famous, and she loved it. She made friends with fellow novelists and intellectuals. She was even famous among the residents of Haworth. But it was not to last. Charlotte married in 1854: having a first child at the age of 38 was hugely risky in those days and she died when three months pregnant.

Immediately after her death, her friend and fellow writer Elizabeth Gaskell began to write *The Life of Charlotte Brontë*. Mrs Gaskell was a successful novelist by trade, not a biographer. She had no intention of spending years on research, and her motivation (apart from the

Two of the outrageous 'Bell brothers' – Anne (left, as painted by 18-year-old Charlotte in 1834) and Charlotte herself, painted after her death by John Hunter Thompson of Bradford, and based on the idealised portrait by the London artist George Richmond

money) was to explain how the three sisters could have written such outrageous novels. She thought she knew the answer even before she started work on the book.

It was the consequence of the Brontës' upbringing: Haworth was a wild and isolated hamlet in the hills, which newspapers never reached, where books and all other cultural activity were unknown, and its people were uncivilised heathens – Yorkshire heathens at that. Elizabeth Gaskell, from the Cheshire side of Manchester, didn't like Yorkshire ways:

> Even an inhabitant of the neighbouring county of Lancaster is struck by the peculiar force of character which the Yorkshire-men display. This makes them interesting as a race; while, at the same time, as individuals, the remarkable degree of self-sufficiency they possess gives them an air of independence rather apt to repel a stranger.

Haworth had begun to be 'inundated with visitors' within two months of the first publication of Mrs Gaskell's book. Nothing has changed!

Moreover, Elizabeth Gaskell believed Charlotte's father Patrick Brontë was eccentric to the point of madness, and had ruled the motherless family with a rod of iron and a vegetarian diet – all of which was quite untrue and came from the malicious gossip of the only servant ever dismissed from the Parsonage.

Much of the book is totally misleading, but it made a great story, and Mrs Gaskell made sure she only consulted sources who would agree with her preconceptions. She also made life easy for herself by quoting extensively but selectively from Charlotte's letters to one particular friend, Ellen Nussey: other sides of the picture are wilfully ignored. Charlotte was presented in the light of a martyr – which is how she had often presented herself, especially to Ellen. The real Charlotte was a much more complicated personality.

Several libel suits followed, but not from those worst libelled, Patrick Brontë and Charlotte's husband Arthur Nicholls.

This book sets out to describe briefly the reality both of the family circle and Haworth at the time. But if you want to get the full picture, you really need to read *The Brontës* by Juliet Barker, a massive work in every respect, which dispels, hopefully for ever, the Brontë myths.

The Rev. Patrick Brontë (1777-1861) shortly before his death. He had outlived all his six children, which must have severely tested his faith

Patrick and Maria Brontë

The Brontë family were from Ireland – where the name was originally Prunty. It seems to have been Patrick's father Hugh who changed it to Brunty. Hugh had a tough life, as a farmer on a small scale in Drumballyroney, County Down, but he was a capable man and was rising in the world. Patrick was one of ten children, and must have been recognised early for his outstanding abilities. He apparently set up a school when he was only 16, and in 1802 entered St John's College, Cambridge as an undergraduate.

Quite how this was achieved is not known. He was a mature student of 25, and he declared his name was not 'Branty', as it had been written in the admissions book, but Brontë – which just happens to be the classical Greek for thunder. It had never been written that way before: in one lightning stroke in the college porters' lodge, a brand was born! Patrick never returned to Ireland.

Despite extreme shortage of funds, he gained his degree and became a clergyman in the Church of England, accepting jobs as a curate in Essex and Shropshire before settling in Yorkshire, where he met his wife-to-be, Maria Branwell who was assisting her aunt in running Woodhouse Grove school. They married in Guiseley on 29 December 1812. Maria was from Penzance in Cornwall, where her family were moderately prosperous grocers in what was then a trading port: their house, 25 Chapel Street, still stands.

7

Thornton's former parsonage is still there, but has an incongruous Victorian front extension which was once a butcher's shop

After a couple of years as curate in Hartshead-cum-Clifton (between Brighouse and Dewsbury), where their first two daughters were born and where Patrick's salary was £65 a year, Patrick and Maria moved to Thornton, to the west of Bradford, where Charlotte (1816), Branwell (1817), Emily (1818) and Anne (1820) were all born.

In 1820, Patrick was appointed to the perpetual curacy of Haworth – a position which in theory was a promotion with increased income, but which was fraught with problems because of disputes between the inhabitants of Haworth and the Vicar of Bradford, a huge parish of which the Haworth curacy was a small part. Genteel poverty would haunt the family for decades to come.

Haworth in the time of the Brontës

Like many West Riding villages, Haworth and the surrounding hamlets had been industrialised from Tudor times, but it was a cottage-based industry. Numerous small-scale farmers, often with minimal landholdings and very poor soil, in fact made most of their living from cloth production whilst keeping a cow and a horse or two, as well as a few pigs and chickens.

These cottages with 'weavers' windows' are in Oxenhope. The area covered by the Haworth curacy in Patrick Brontë's day was huge, including Oxenhope as well as Stanbury and a wide stretch of moorland

The Piece Hall in Halifax. Here individual weavers each had a room from which to sell their cloth – but by the 1820s mechanisation had reduced its importance. The buyers went direct to the mill-owners

The entire family, including children from the age of four or five, would be involved in the various processes, such as sorting, washing, carding or combing, spinning and weaving. A finished 'piece' of cloth might then be taken over the hills by packhorse to the weekly Halifax cloth market, held from 1779 in the magnificent Piece Hall.

Much of the Haworth worsted industry was organised by local families such as the Greenwoods and Heatons, who sent their agents as far afield as Giggleswick and Sawley to leave the raw material with cottage spinners and collect it a few weeks later, to be delivered to other cottagers for weaving in the Haworth area. The Greenwoods and Heatons then traded direct with London merchants, and even as far afield as St Petersburg.

Vale Mills at Oakworth, originally built around 1785 but much enlarged in the 1850s. Notice the river running under the mill

By 1820 the cloth industry was changing fast. Soon the old hand-loom weavers could no longer make a living, because of the new mechanised mills. The earliest mills – dating from about 1785 in Haworth – produced cotton textiles. As a new industry, cotton may have provided welcome extra jobs, but before long mechanisation was applied to woollens and worsted.

The mills employed many women and children, but very few men. In 1851 the Springhead and Lees mills apparently employed between them 83 boys, 93 girls, 222 women and just four men – and the men were the four Merrall brothers who owned the mills. The price of finished cloth fell, and the cottage handloom weavers could no longer make a living. Huge discontent led to the Luddite riots in 1812 and the Plug Riots of 1842, but these were just moments when the simmering discontent burst out in violence. Fear of riot and even revolution was always present.

Haworth itself was not a major manufacturing centre because of inadequate transport links – no canal, no railway and poor roads – and also because it lacked good quality local coal. Its mills continued

Spring Head Mill, just north of Haworth village, originally built by Joseph Greenwood, and bought by Hartley Merrall in 1829. The mill complex has now been converted into housing

The mill-owner's house at Spring Head, very near the mill but a world away in living conditions

to rely on water power when others were upgrading to steam. The fluctuations of trade affected all mills. Mill owners might make their fortunes, and they certainly lived a very different lifestyle from their workforce, but it was not unusual for them to go bankrupt. They were a tight-fisted breed, but even if they had been more inclined to be generous to their workers, their businesses might not have been able to sustain higher wages except in boom times.

The consequences in Haworth, as for many other places in Yorkshire and Lancashire, included poverty, astoundingly awful living conditions, and child labour. There were 25 households living below street level in two-room cellars. Large, solid back-to-backs, such as those opposite the station which were built around 1880, would have seemed like palaces to the mill workers of the Brontë period.

Patrick Brontë was very active in trying to improve water supply and sanitation, but was opposed by the wealthy parish ratepayers who were expected to foot the bill. An 1851 report by an Inspector of the Board of Health, brought in by Patrick, described 'middensteads' (heaps of human dung) everywhere in the village, no covered drains or sewers, no water closets, and on average one earth privy for every four houses. And in the slum areas, all now demolished of course, it was even worse: in two cases 24 houses shared one privy.

The water supply was almost certainly polluted. The average life expectancy in Haworth village, for those who survived their first year, was 25.8 years, as bad as the worst parts of London or Liverpool.

In the mills a 69 hour working week (12 hours a day with a mere 9 hours on Saturday) was the norm, but in good times 16 hours a day was possible, and in bad times the workers were laid off without pay. In theory the Factory Act of 1802 had prohibited the employment of children under nine years old, and required factory owners to provide schools for them. It was ignored. The 1833 Factory Act was better publicised, but the magistrates who should have enforced it were often mill owners themselves, and that Act too was ignored.

The 1833 Act had been opposed locally. Hartley Merrall, for example, agreed with a Bingley surgeon that the hours were not excessive, and that children did not need recreation. The minister of the West Street Baptist Chapel opposed the Act, and quite probably so did many of the poorest families. After all, if the menfolk were out of work, the family needed income from the children if it was to survive – which is perhaps one reason why the population of Haworth shot up between 1801 and 1851. There are certainly many working children shown in the 1851 census, including an 8-year-old worsted spinner living two doors from the Parsonage, and several other 8-year-old 'factory operatives'.

For a visitor to Haworth today there is no evidence of the extreme hardships suffered by ordinary people in early Victorian times. Perhaps more significantly, those hardships might well come as a surprise to readers of the Brontë novels. No reader of Dickens, or Mrs Gaskell, could be unaware of the poverty which was so near the surface even in polite areas, but (with a few half-hearted and unconvincing exceptions by Charlotte) the realities of industrial life as it affected the poor are utterly ignored by all three sisters.

The Keighley & Worth Valley Railway was opened in 1867, and the back-to-backs opposite the station are later still. Sanitary reformers wrongly believed that diseases were caused by bad air, rather than contagious germs: back-to-backs had poor air circulation, so were wrongly blamed for cholera and other diseases

In *Agnes Grey*, a family is reduced to the terrible hardship of having to do their own gardening, and has only one maidservant, though Anne Brontë does point to the sparing use of coal, and to threadbare clothes and carpets, which were the nearest her own family came to poverty. As for child labour, the only reference is in Charlotte's novel *Shirley*:

> It was eight o'clock; the mill lights were all extinguished; the children, released for half an hour from toil, betook themselves to the little tin cans which held their coffee, and to the small baskets which contained their allowance of bread.
> Let's hope they have enough to eat; it would be a pity were it otherwise.

A pity indeed. The achievements of the Brontë sisters were huge, but not in the area of 'the social novel'. It is rather ironic that they are so closely associated with Haworth, when they seem to have been strangely oblivious of its people.

For those with leisure, like the Brontë sisters, the moors were a place to escape the prevailing smells of smoke and open sewers. The dot on the horizon at the centre of this photo is Top Withens

In 1905, Whiteley Turner researched *A Spring-Time Saunter round and about Brontë-Land*, which was published in 1913. He interviewed many local people with memories of the family ('yar' in this passage is 'our'):

> Na, yo know we (turning to her husband) can't remember th' Brontës, but iv heeard mi muther tell abaat when my father en her used ta be sizin' and stretchin' ther warps et th'bottom o'th'moor, near Wattery-loin top – ya know yar fooaks wer handloom weeavers – theease Brontë lasses used to cum past when art fer a walk. They'd a bein eeather readin' a bouk, er dooin' sum mak o' fancy wark. They wod walk on jest es if ther'wornt a soul i'th'rooad, en never lift ther eyes nor speeak a word tiv yar fooaks, nor tiv onybody they met; but 'E suppoose it wer' ther waa.

It was indeed their way, though the three sisters were each very different in character, and it is worth reading the novels in that light.

The Brontës' childhood

Patrick and Maria Brontë and their six young children arrived in Haworth in April 1820, to live in the attractive Parsonage at the very top of the village. True, the graveyard does loom large, but at that time – before the wing facing the car park and then the museum shop building had been added – many of the rooms looked out over open countryside. Whilst the original house is smaller than the frontage suggests, and by modern standards must have been cramped for a family of that size, it was spacious compared with all other housing in the area, except the grand houses of the gentry and some mill owners. What's more, it was provided rent-free to the curate. Patrick and Maria must have been thrilled.

However, before a year was up Maria was ill with cancer, and in September 1821 she died, aged 38, with her six children (the eldest aged seven) and her husband and sister Elizabeth all lined up at the bedside to bid her farewell.

It was a financial as well as an emotional and housekeeeping crisis. Maria had been receiving an annuity which was a significant part of the household income, now lost. Elizabeth ('Aunt Branwell') wanted to get back to her native Cornwall. Patrick in his desperation wrote a businesslike letter proposing marriage to a wealthy young lady with whom he was acquainted. She was furious. He proposed to another wealthy acquaintance, and was rejected, then tried writing to an old flame whom he had abandoned fifteen years earlier – and received an appropriate rebuff.

The obvious answer was to propose to Elizabeth Branwell, but under canon law it was not permissible to marry a deceased wife's sister. This was not enshrined in civil law until 1835 (rescinded 1907): Jane Austen's brother and the famous engineering entrepreneur Matthew Boulton each married his deceased wife's sister. But as a clergyman, Patrick could not marry Elizabeth.

The upshot was that Patrick remained a widower and 'Aunt Branwell' stayed on, as housekeeper, for the remaining twenty years of her life. It would be surprising if she did not feel deep down that her life had been hijacked. Whilst Mrs Gaskell's picture of the Brontës' childhood is certainly unfair, and both Patrick and Elizabeth used their best efforts to give the children a secure and loving home life, the impression remains that perhaps neither of them was a particularly warm personality, and both had to try quite hard.

The children, on the other hand, bonded together deeply and naturally, rather to the exclusion of outsiders. As Charlotte put it:

> Resident in a remote district in which education had made little progress, and where consequently there was little inducement to seek social intercourse beyond our own domestic circle, we were wholly dependent on ourselves and each other.

They played together in the house, and walked out onto the moors which started at the back of the garden. At a very early age, they began to create communal make-believe worlds. It may have been a strange household, but the children were happy within their cocoon.

However, they needed an education. If the five girls were to move in the right kind of society with a view to marriage, or failing that to the only permissible career for a spinster, teaching, whether as a governess or in a private school, they needed to learn how to conduct themselves; and Branwell would need to prepare for a career of some kind. But schooling had to be paid for, and Patrick could not really afford it.

Suddenly a new school opened, run as a charity especially for the daughters of clergymen. It had a number of illustrious patrons, and looked absolutely perfect for the purpose. In 1824 Maria, Elizabeth and Charlotte were taken the 45 miles (72 km) to the Clergy Daughters School at Cowan Bridge, which is on the A65 between Ingleton and Kirkby Lonsdale, and Emily followed a few months later.

No one who has read *Jane Eyre* can forget Charlotte's picture of life there, with inedible food, bitter cold, and treatment that verges on the sadistic, often in the name of religion. Much of that description is probably accurate, but it is deliberately presented through the eyes of an unhappy and lonely child, torn from her home and hating the fact that she is an object of charity. No doubt Charlotte found it cathartic to express her bitterness. In fact, Cowan Bridge was in many ways typical of boarding schools of that time.

It was certainly typical in that some of the pupils died from contagious diseases, partly caused by insanitary conditions, but also inevitable in boarding school communities at a time when the diseases were not understood, and little could be done to prevent them. Children often died at home too. The girls at Cowan Bridge were taught how to die a good death, repenting their sins and showing confidence in the mercy of the Lord.

The two eldest Brontë sisters, Maria and Elizabeth, succumbed to TB (tuberculosis, in those days called 'consumption') while the rest of the school was enduring an outbreak of typhus. They were separately sent back to Haworth where they died within six weeks of each other. Patrick rushed off to collect Charlotte (just turned nine years old) and Emily (six) and bring them back, at the beginning of June 1825, to the protection of home.

The teenage years

For the next five years there was no more schooling, other than that provided by Patrick and Aunt Branwell. The make-believe worlds became ever more important, with Branwell and Charlotte immersed in 'Glasstown' and then 'Angria', and Emily and Anne in 'Gondal'. In the course of their imaginings they produced a huge number of miniature books, in a tiny script based on print. Much of the content was highly derivative, based on their voracious reading of novels, poetry and periodicals such as *Blackwell's Magazine*.

These collaborative imaginative games continued even into their adult lives, especially in the case of Emily. It was simultaneously a strength and a weakness, the way in which they learned the writer's craft but perhaps also a way of fending off reality. If as adults they ignored their neighbours while out walking, it was probably not because they were rude (though Charlotte was certainly a snob) but because they were totally engaged in another world, an imaginative world fuelled by authors we no longer read, such as Scott, Byron, 'Monk' Lewis and the German Romantic writers. Other people, in the 'real' world, simply did not exist.

Gondal and Angria had the same kind of hold over them as computer worlds have on some teenagers today. They might even have been familiar with the word avatar. Walter Scott described Napoleon escaping from St Helena as 'a third avatar of this singular emanation of the Evil Principle'.

The Napoleonic wars were a major inspiration for the imaginary worlds of the Brontës, and the Duke of Wellington and his brother Arthur Wellesley, lightly disguised, were among the characters

The Red House at Gomershall, childhood home of Charlotte's lifelong friend Mary Taylor, which features as 'Briarmains' in 'Shirley'

deployed. Romantic themes were as important as the military and political, and Charlotte's male avatar the Duke of Zamorna was a cynical Byronic adulterer. Needless to say, in imaginative games children always envisage themselves as the leaders of society, powerful, wealthy, aristocratic and above convention – and this was the end of the Regency period, after all, when for male aristocrats, and not a few females, sexual freedom was the norm. It was Wellington himself who, approached by a blackmailer with a kiss-and-tell story, replied 'Publish and be damned!' In the 1820s, only the merchant classes tried to hide such things. Victorian prudery had yet to make its impact.

If imaginary world role-play continues beyond childhood, the constraints of real life may perhaps be felt as tiresome, unpleasant or deeply unfair. Patrick Brontë himself did not approve of make-believe worlds, or indeed of novels, and in one of his own moralistic published stories wrote:

> The sensual novelist and his admirer are beings of depraved appetites and sickly imaginations, who having the art of *self-tormenting* are diligently and zealously employed in creating an imaginary world, which they can never inhabit, only to make the real world, with which they must necessarily be conversant, gloomy and insupportable.

Children educated at home in a bookish household often acquire knowledge far more wide-ranging than their contemporaries, and the Brontës certainly had that experience. The downside can be that such children may lack intellectual discipline, but the greatest danger is that they do not learn to socialise.

All three of the girls had serious health problems whenever they had to leave home, which repeatedly forced them to return to the safety of the Parsonage. Many of those episodes appear to have been psychological, with depression turning into very real physical illness.

In 1831, when Charlotte was 14, she was finally sent back to school, Roe Head School, at Mirfield between Huddersfield and Dewsbury. It was run by a Miss Wooler, and was a school for the daughters of gentlefolk. The fees must have stretched Patrick's budget, but it brought Charlotte into contact with girls who would remain her friends for life – as indeed did Miss Wooler herself. Charlotte made a strange initial impression. Mary Taylor wrote:

> I first saw her coming out of a covered cart, in very old-fashioned clothes, and looking very cold and miserable. She was coming to school at Miss Wooler's. When she appeared in the schoolroom, her dress was changed, but just as old. She looked a little old woman, so short-sighted that she always appeared to be seeking something, and moving her head from side to side to catch a sight of it. She was very shy and nervous, and spoke with a strong Irish accent. When a book was given her, she dropped her head over it till her nose nearly touched it, and when she was told to hold her head up, up went the book after it, still close to her nose, so that it was not possible to help laughing.

Charlotte was always very sensitive about her looks and her short stature (she described herself as 'stunted') as well as conscious of her relative poverty. The fact that her family was at the very bottom of the gentry pecking order was far more important to her than the fact that the gentry were the top 5% of the social hierarchy. She described the factory workers among whom she lived in Haworth as 'peasants', and in her writing treats them almost as subhuman. But to be fair, living in worn-out clothes and other people's cast-offs, when their friends could afford the latest fashions, or travelling in a carrier's cart when

Top: Ponden Hall, home of the Heaton family, with whom the Brontës were friendly. It has been suggested as the original for Thrushcross Grange, but Emily was surely capable of combining many inspirations – literary as well as real – when creating settings for her novels

Below: Kildwick Hall, described in the 1820s as 'the seat of Miss Currer'. The girls may have known it, but this was the gentry world to which they could only aspire

other families had their own carriage and pair, would have depressed most teenage girls.

The suggestion that she had an Irish accent is interesting. In such a reclusive household the accents of Patrick (Irish) and Maria and then Elizabeth (Cornish) may have had more influence than if the family had been more outgoing. Given the anti-Irish prejudice of the times, Charlotte later tended to hide her Irish ancestry, though Branwell may perhaps have embraced his with a macho swagger: in the 1841 Census return, his entry is 'corrected' to show his place of birth as Ireland, when in fact he was born in Yorkshire.

Roe Head was in many respects a good school, and Charlotte flourished there, both in her studies and in her social life. She was there for 18 months, probably all Patrick could afford, and in 1832 returned home to supervise her sisters' education.

Out into the world

In 1836 everything changed. The next few years were a hectic whirl, as the Brontës launched themselves on the world, and repeatedly fell back to earth with a thud.

Branwell set out to be a portrait painter. After taking lessons from a professional, he rented rooms and a studio in Bradford but, unsurprisingly, although he was quite talented he could not make it pay. Then he became a private tutor in Broughton-in-Furness at the southern end of the Lake District, but was dismissed, probably for getting a local servant girl pregnant.

Almost immediately he found himself a job on the newly opened Leeds & Manchester Railway, won promotion as clerk-in-charge at Luddenden Foot station, then was dismissed because the accounts were in a mess and a sum of money was unaccounted for. Meanwhile he began to get his poetry published in magazines.

Charlotte returned to Roe Head in 1835 as a teacher. Emily accompanied her as a pupil – in effect going to school for the first time at the age of 17, with her fees paid for out of Charlotte's salary. Imposed routines, rote learning and living in close proximity to other girls were a nightmare to her. As Charlotte said, 'Liberty was the breath of Emily's nostrils, without it she perished.' I suspect that someone like Emily might today be pigeon-holed, 'autistic spectrum disorder' or some such label. Within a couple of months she was seriously ill, and returned home, to resume her diet of Sir Walter Scott and walks on the moors. Anne took her place and probably was equally miserable, but felt it her duty to stay.

Charlotte soon knew she hated teaching, especially pretending to be patient when she was raging internally at the 'most asinine stupidity of these fatheaded oafs'. Especially when the sun was shining in the imaginary world of Angria. Both sisters seem to have gone through a phase of morbid religiosity, believing themselves damned. Anne fell ill, and did not return to the school after the Christmas holidays of 1837. Charlotte returned, succumbed to what she called 'the tyranny of Hypochondria', and resigned. Only to return three months later, and resign again.

Emily took a job teaching, but after six months became ill and gave up. Anne took a job as a governess, and was dismissed, probably because she could not control spoilt brats.

Charlotte too then became a governess, which she found even worse than school teaching. A governess was neither part of the family, nor a servant: it was a lonely role, and the Brontë novels, especially *Agnes Grey*, reveal its horrors to the full. In Charlotte's case she seems to have been hypersensitive to what she regarded as snubs, and indeed to have gone out of her way to irritate her employers – especially the woman of the household, while believing that the husband could do no wrong. Both Charlotte's attempts at being a governess were failures.

Anne quickly got another job as a governess at Thorp Green Hall, near York, with the Rev. Edmund Robinson and his wife – a position in which she seems to have been greatly appreciated by both children and parents. In her case determination won through over loneliness.

Charlotte and Emily decided that the only way forward for them was to open a school themselves. This would require capital, in which their aunt might be able to help, but it also required them to have more advanced skills. Borrowing money from their aunt, they embarked on an extraordinarily brave venture – and enrolled at a school in Brussels as pupils. The school was run by a Mme Heger. In those days university education was not available to women, and per-haps this trip should be seen as its equivalent. They left in February 1842, returning urgently in November when Aunt Branwell died, which of course changed the household entirely.

Emily was delighted to take on the role of housekeeper at the Parsonage, and a visitor remembered Emily kneading dough in the kitchen with a German language book propped open in front of her. Scope for her imagination, her own chosen routines, a beloved dog and walks on the moors were what kept Emily sane.

Aunt Branwell had left each of the three girls a legacy of £300, and this made the school project more attainable. Charlotte headed back to Brussels – but not just to improve her French and German and to do some teaching in order to pay for her own lessons. She was besot-ted with Monsieur Heger, who taught at his wife's school as well as at other establishments. Charlotte was not good at concealing her feel-ings, and Mme Heger must soon have noticed.

Monsieur Heger did not succumb. Charlotte demonised Mme Heger in her own mind, and since she despised pretty well everyone in the school apart from her beloved Master she had a dismal time of it,

Time and time again the four young Brontës' attempts to earn their own living failed, and they returned to Haworth

and doubtless made other people's lives a misery with her sulking. In the end she took the decision to return home, but continued writing passionate letters to M. Heger for some time to come.

Aspects of this experience are of course present in the novels. When Jane Eyre leaves Mr Rochester after the thwarted wedding, Charlotte Brontë knows precisely how she feels. But having your rival declared insane, locked in an attic and burned to death is a solution only open to novelists – perhaps fortunately for Mme Heger.

Meanwhile Branwell had joined Anne at Thorp Green Hall to be tutor to the boys of the family, and would be there for more than two years. Charlotte and Emily had a prospectus prepared for a school within the Parsonage. They failed to enrol even a single pupil and, probably to the relief of the whole household, soon abandoned the project. By this time Patrick's sight was failing, and he was lucky to find a new and particularly helpful curate, Arthur Bell Nicholls. Like many of Patrick's assistants, Arthur was Irish.

The Black Bull became a second home for Branwell after his dismissal from the Robinsons. He was a talented young man, but as a friend said, 'he was just a man moving in a mist, who lost his way'

Suddenly in June 1845 Anne, who had seemed totally settled, resigned from her job and came home, without offering any explanation. In July, Branwell followed her, but he had been dismissed. It seems that Branwell was discovered to be having an affair with Mrs Robinson, whose husband was an invalid.

Given the age difference, we might nowadays describe him as her toy-boy, but from his reaction we can have no doubt that Branwell was as madly in love with Mrs Robinson as Charlotte was with Monsieur Heger. To Charlotte's disgust, Branwell let everyone know about his woes. He began to drink himself to death, funded by large sums of money brought by messengers from Thorp Green, presumably to buy his silence. When Mr Robinson died, Mrs Robinson pretended that his will prevented her from remarrying – dashing Branwell's romantic hopes: she soon moved to Birmingham and married Sir Edward Scott.

All four young Brontës were now back at home, their careers in ruins.

Literary ambitions

Branwell had already had poetry published in magazines, and he now decided to write a novel. He realised there was no money to be made in poetry, though it was widely seen as a higher form of literature. The girls, by contrast, gathered together their poetry and decided to publish it themselves: self-publishing was quite common then, as it is again now, and authors were often deluded into expecting success. *Poems by Currer, Ellis and Acton Bell* was published on 6 May 1846, and sold just two copies.

All three girls, but particularly Emily, wanted anonymity, partly because they felt that women's writing was treated with condescension by reviewers and they wanted to be judged by the same standard as men. Their pseudonyms were probably taken from the surnames of three intellectual women they admired, Frances Mary Richardson Currer, a Yorkshire philanthropist whom Charlotte may have met, Elizabeth Acton, now famous only for her excellent cookery book but also a poet whom Anne may have admired, and Sarah Stickney Ellis, who wrote about the education of women, and herself set up a school. As for 'Bell', it might have been from the educationist Dr Andrew Bell – but I think it more likely the girls were simply inspired by the new peal of bells installed in Haworth church while they were preparing their book. (Tennyson's poem 'Ring out wild Bells' was alas not written till 1850!)

They had to admit that Branwell was right in thinking writing fiction was a better way of making money than self-publishing poetry, and promptly each started writing a novel.

Charlotte used her Brussels experience for *The Professor*, marred by a clumsy attempt to write about Yorkshire mill-owners and by using a male narrator's voice. Emily wrote *Wuthering Heights*, a story very much in the Gondal manner, in a timeless world, with more than a touch of Sir Walter Scott and few concessions to 'reality'. And Anne wrote *Agnes Grey*, a quiet novel about a very ordinary young woman, with its rather too overt moral commentary interrupting the flow, but attacking some very real aspects of contemporary society which Anne had observed as a governess. There are ghastly parents giving children too much freedom, permitting or even encouraging them to be cruel to animals and people, shirking parental responsibility and expecting

Haworth Parsonage, home to the Brontës from 1820, now a museum

the governess to compensate. The clergy too are attacked for their deference to wealth and power.

Then as now, getting a first novel published by a reputable company was not easy. The manuscripts went the round of London publishers. Anne and Emily were in time prepared to accept terms from a less than respectable publisher called Newby – but in effect they had to pay him for the printing, so it was self-publishing again.

Charlotte presumably refused this route. She received a very complimentary letter from Smith, Elder & Co, turning down *The Professor* but giving cogent reasons and hoping the author would send them any future novel. Such letters even in those days were unusual – publishers don't have the time to respond thoughtfully to the hundreds of unsolicited manuscripts they receive.

When she received the letter from Smith, Elder & Co, the three Brontë novels had been circulating round London for almost a year, enough time back in Haworth to write a second novel, and *Jane Eyre*, much of it inspired by a trip to Hathersage in Derbyshire, was only a month from completion. Charlotte pressed ahead. She despatched the manuscript on 24 August 1847 and it caused a sensation at Smith, Elder & Co. Within eight weeks it was published.

It is a book which glows with intensity, and it seems to have come easily to her. She later wrote to G H Lewes:

> When authors write best, or, at least, when they write most fluently, an influence seems to waken in them, which becomes their master – which will have its own way – putting out of view all behests but its own, dictating certain words, and insisting on their being used, whether vehement or measured in their nature; new-moulding characters, giving unthought-of turns to incidents, rejecting carefully elaborated old ideas, and suddenly creating and adopting new ones.

That certainly applied to the writing of *Jane Eyre*. The use of a first-person female narrator, and the autobiographical experiences she drew on, make it difficult to distinguish what is 'Jane' from what is Charlotte – but that is what gives the book its power. It is full of passionate indignation, not that the world is full of injustice, but that the injustice is happening *to me*! The reader can hardly avoid becoming involved with the child Jane Eyre.

And for some at least of its female readers, Jane's passion for Mr Rochester is equally something to which they can uncritically relate. The review in *The Quarterly* (written anonymously and cattily by Elizabeth Rigby, soon to be the wife of the Director of the National Gallery) is frequently hilarious in its outdated cultural assumptions, but it is also extremely perceptive in many ways (and worth seeking out on-line). It points out that:

> Mr Rochester is a man who deliberately and secretly seeks to violate the laws of both God and man, and yet we will be bound half our lady readers are enchanted with him for a model of generosity and honour. We would have thought that such a hero had no chance, in the purer taste of the present day; but the popularity of *Jane Eyre* is a proof how deeply the love for illegitimate romance is implanted in our nature…

> Still we say again this is a very remarkable book. We are painfully alive to the moral, religious and literary deficiencies of the picture, and such passages of beauty and power as we have quoted cannot redeem it, but it is impossible not to be spellbound with the freedom of the touch. It would be mere hackneyed courtesy to call it 'fine writing'. It bears no impress

of being written at all but is poured out rather in the heat and hurry of an instinct, which flows ungovernably on to its object, indifferent by what means it reaches it, and unconscious too.

A book that casts such a spell over a reviewer who thinks she ought to hate its every word is clearly best-seller material – and so it proved.

Literary success

The huge and immediate success of *Jane Eyre* finally goaded Thomas Newby into publishing *Wuthering Heights* and *Agnes Grey*. The latter was ignored by the reviewers, but *Wuthering Heights* attracted their interest – even if they could not decide what to make of it. The absence of any kind of moral in the tale, indeed the absence of any moral structure in the universe it described, was puzzling and disturbing to the reviewers, but one wrote that 'if the rank of a work of fiction is to depend solely on its naked imaginative power, then this is one of the greatest novels in the language.' It is a question which has divided readers of Emily Brontë ever since.

Both Emily and Anne agreed terms with Newby for their second novels, and Anne's *The Tenant of Wildfell Hall* was published in June 1848. Its subject matter intensified the attacks on the 'coarse Bell brothers' as being obsessed with vicious and debauched behaviour.

The theme is the plight of a woman whose husband has given himself up to drunkenness and bad company, and her right (not then at all accepted by society) to leave him and take her child away too. It was probably inspired by the experiences of a Mrs Collins, who had poured out her heart to the Brontës, and whose husband was actually a clergyman.

To modern eyes it seems a highly moral story, and Anne was certainly conscientiously religious, but religious attitudes change over time. Many people then believed that sweeping nasty facts under the carpet was vital, so that they did not corrupt innocent minds. To Anne the misunderstanding must have been galling, but the hostile reviews were great publicity. Sales were excellent!

However, the new book had a more immediate consequence. Thomas Newby sold sheets to an American publisher at a high price by fraudulently suggesting the book was by 'Currer Bell'. Charlotte and Anne packed overnight bags and left for London the same day

The ruins of Top Withens, whose remote setting may have been an inspiration for 'Wuthering Heights'

they heard of this, to make sure that their publishers (but not the outside world) knew the truth. At Smith, Elder & Co, George Smith pretended astonishment, but it is hard to believe that such an astute man had not already guessed that 'Currer Bell' was the Miss Brontë to whom all correspondence had to be addressed. George Smith later wrote:

> I must confess that my first impression of Charlotte Brontë's personal appearance was that it was interesting rather than attractive. She was very small and had a quaint old-fashioned look. Her head seemed too large for her body. She had fine eyes, but her face was marred by the shape of her mouth and by the complexion. There was but little feminine charm about her; and of this fact she was uneasily and perpetually conscious. It may seem strange that the possession of genius did not lift her above the weakness of an excessive anxiety about her personal appearance. But I believe she would have given all her genius and her fame to have been beautiful
>
> Perhaps few women ever existed more anxious to be pretty than she, or more angrily conscious of the circumstance that she was *not* pretty.

There followed a whirlwind of entertainment, including an evening at the opera. No details survive of their confrontation with Mr Newby.

Charlotte now tried to focus on her third novel, *Shirley*. It is set around 1812, at the time of the Luddite riots, and Charlotte clearly felt she ought to be writing a 'social novel', rather than reworking her limited personal experiences, and that she must avoid that 'brutalising influence of unchecked passion' for which 'the Bell brothers' were by now notorious.

It was a mistake. The only social question in which she was truly interested was that of women's role in the world and their career opportunities – an important enough question, but one cannot help feeling the only reason she was interested was that it was her own plight. If Charlotte had been born into a wealthy family, able to write and travel widely without having to work, she would have cared little about the fate of less well-placed women – any more than she could be bothered with the real experience of working people. She pored over old newspapers to study the Luddite riots, while totally ignoring the very similar poverty, suffering, unrest and protest meetings which were happening on her doorstep in 1848, the year the Chartist movement was crushed.

Domestic disaster

The most remarkable thing about *Shirley* is that it was ever completed at all, because a terrible sequence of events now struck the Parsonage. Branwell died on 29 September 1848, aged 31. Though weakened by alcoholism, he probably actually died of TB. Emily succumbed to TB and died ten weeks later. Before long it was clear that Anne was ill too. She died on a trip to her beloved Scarborough the following May, and Charlotte arranged for her to be buried there.

In such circumstances it is astonishing that Charlotte could write at all. If *Shirley* seems to change course part way through, that is no doubt the reason. It was received respectfully rather than enthusiastically. The loss of her sisters meant there was now no reason for Charlotte to remain anonymous – and she had no wish to. By the end of 1849 she was visiting London, meeting her literary hero Thackeray, and flirting with the handsome George Smith, eight years younger than her. She was back in London again the following May, which was when her portrait was drawn by George Richmond: he was renowned

for his ability to flatter his clients, and there is little doubt that his portrait of Charlotte does just that.

Suddenly Charlotte was famous in her own right, not just as Currer Bell. She could meet her fellow authors on equal terms, and socialise with intellectuals. She went on visits to the homes of Elizabeth Gaskell and Harriet Martineau, and returned to London to see the Great Exhibition. She even visited Edinburgh with George Smith (and his mother) on what became a Sir Walter Scott tour. Amidst all this new and exciting activity she somehow managed to write *Villette*, which drew once again upon her Brussels experience but also upon her friendship with George Smith, who appears as Dr John Bretton. Many serious critics regard *Villette* as Charlotte's finest work, full of the same kind of passion as *Jane Eyre* but more mature in treatment, and it received very good reviews on its publication.

Charlotte's fictional characters were often based on close observation of real people, and this had already caused problems locally with *Shirley*. To people in Birstall and Gomersall, the portraits were all too lifelike, and they tried to identify 'Currer Bell'. Now that she was known, many more people would be able to identify such characters, including those of George Smith and his mother in *Villette*, and would draw their own conclusions about what might have happened in real life. And what would George himself think? Charlotte hesitated – but the artist in her won, and the manuscript was despatched on 20 November 1852.

As a businessman, George Smith knew he needed to publish the latest novel by his bestselling author: as an individual, he must have hated it. The businessman in him won, but the relationship with Charlotte cooled. On his side, it had probably never been serious.

At around this time Charlotte allowed Smith, Elder & Co to reissue *Wuthering Heights* and *Agnes Grey*, but not *The Tenant of Wildfell Hall*, which 'it hardly appears to me desirable to preserve'. At the same time she published some of her sisters' poetry, but chopping and changing it editorially in the most disgraceful manner, often quite altering the meaning. There is also reason to believe that she may have destroyed the manuscript of a second novel by Emily.

She probably told herself she was preserving her sisters' reputation, but today it looks more as though she was preserving her own – against the prudish critics, and perhaps against works which might distract or even detract from her own achievements. *The Tenant of Wildfell Hall*, in particular, might have been a serious competitor.

If Elizabeth Gaskell painted Charlotte as a saint and martyr, it may be thought I am doing the opposite! True, I do believe she was in many ways a selfish, certainly a self-centred person – but then many creative people are: successful creativity demands self-belief and determination, often at the expense of the artist's immediate family, who are expected to devote themselves to its support and nurture. In Charlotte's case, it is precisely the intense presentation of her own self-belief which characterises her best work – and with which we as readers gladly identify.

Romance at last?

For years Charlotte and her friend Ellen Nussey had been discussing the likelihood that they would become 'old maids'. Given that she was clearly plain, and without wealth, it may come as a surprise to hear that by the time *Villette* was published Charlotte had received and rejected four proposals of marrriage. In 1839 Ellen's brother, the Rev.

Henry Nussey, had obtained a curacy in Sussex, intended to start a school, and sent Charlotte an eminently sensible letter suggesting she marry him and look after his pupils. It was this incident which inspired the St John Rivers proposal in *Jane Eyre*. Only a few months later, a visiting Irish-born curate met her just once, fell passionately in love at first sight, and the next day proposed by letter. Then in 1851, the Managing Clerk of Smith, Elder & Co called at Haworth on a similar mission, but he was about to go to India on behalf of the firm, and in any case Charlotte found him too self-assertive.

Her financial future was never fully secure, but she was not prepared to marry for security alone, and she seems to have rejected these three suitors without any self-doubts.

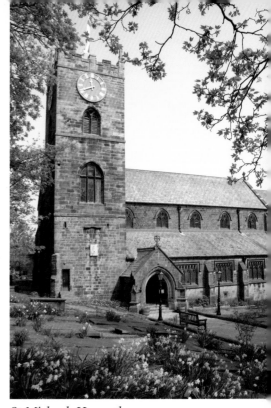

St Michael, Haworth, was largely rebuilt in the 1870s

The fourth was a different matter. Arthur Bell Nicholls had been curate under Patrick for seven years, and suddenly in December 1852, while *Villette* was in production, he proposed to Charlotte, without having asked Patrick's permission first. Before Charlotte could decide for herself, Patrick exploded and Charlotte was forced to refuse. Arthur, who normally repressed his emotions, was visibly shattered and resigned his job, with no other prospects.

Perhaps Patrick's outrageous behaviour influenced Charlotte, or perhaps it was the souring of her fantasy relationship with George Smith, but she soon began to regret Arthur's departure. She herself became ill, and then Patrick suffered a stroke, his second.

Charlotte started a clandestine correspondence with Arthur. Within the Parsonage, what Charlotte wanted, Charlotte usually got. In time she forced her father to accept that she would marry Arthur, and she forced Arthur to accept that they must live at the Parsonage to look after her father.

The wedding was at 8 o'clock in the morning of Thursday, 29 June 1854 with scarcely anyone in the village aware of the event. The couple took their honeymoon in Ireland, visiting his relations – who to her astonishment turned out to be both wealthy and genteel. (Charlotte had no intention of contacting her own relations in Drumballyroney, who were neither.)

When they returned to Haworth, for the first time ever Charlotte took a delight in helping in parish affairs. She was blissfully happy in her marriage – and her letters to Ellen suggested she no longer had much time to spare for her old friend. Arthur was to be the sole object of her attention. Ellen must have been deeply hurt.

Before long, Charlotte was pregnant, suffering what seemed to be 'morning sickness'. Soon she was 'completely prostrated with weakness and sickness and constant fever.' She died on 31 March 1855, aged 38.

Arthur stayed at the Parsonage and looked after his father-in-law. He also made possible the publication of Charlotte's first novel, *The Professor*. Arthur and Patrick did their best to cooperate with Elizabeth Gaskell, whose *Life of Charlotte Brontë* was published in March 1857, but Mrs Gaskell's view of them both was poisoned by Ellen Nussey, for whom 'bitter and twisted' seems a reasonable description.

When Patrick died in June 1861, his post as curate should have gone to Arthur, who had done most of the parish work for the previous decade. For reasons which remain obscure, the church trustees voted narrowly against him. He retreated to Ireland, where in time he married a cousin but, with his new wife's acquiescence, maintained their home as a Brontë shrine.

Haworth, meanwhile, was also in the process of becoming a literary pilgrimage destination second only to Stratford. The opening of the Keighley & Worth Valley Railway in 1867 linked Haworth to the national rail network, making it much more accessible, and the steam train from Keighley or Oxenhope remains the quintessential way to reach it today.

The Parsonage Museum allows us to appreciate something of the family's domestic situation, and is full of fascinating memorabilia.

For a sense of the landscape which inspired all three sisters, but especially Emily, the classic walk out onto the moors and up to Top Withens is a must – but it's a long walk and you need to go prepared. See page 40 for information about Top Withens.

West Lane, built in 1844, is one of two Baptist churches in the village. Many of Patrick Brontë's problems arose because the majority of his parishioners were nonconformists, who were nevertheless required to pay tithes and church rates to support the Church of England. This created a very understandable resentment and there were some unedifying rows

One of Haworth's oldest buildings is this former farm in North Road, which is probably seventeenth century despite its doorway in a style characteristic of the Tudor period

The village of Stanbury, to the west of Haworth, lies on what was once an important transpennine route between Bradford and Colne

The Keighley & Worth Valley Railway

The invention of railways revolutionised transport in Britain, with both canals and roads suddenly appearing obsolete. Without a railway, industries were at a major disadvantage. Leeds had the railway in 1840, Bradford 1846, Keighley by 1847.

As early as 1845, a proposal for a line from Hebden Bridge via Oxenhope and Haworth to Keighley was supported by Patrick Brontë as well as by the local mill-owners. Branwell even applied for the post as Secretary to the new company – but didn't get the job. Just at the wrong time, the railway share bubble burst, and the company folded without the line being built.

It was not until 1867 that the Keighley & Worth Valley Railway was finally opened, and then only as a branch line, 5 miles (8 km) long. It was mainly funded by the mill owners, but before long was taken over by the Midland Railway. As a branch line it was inevitably targeted by Dr Beeching and was closed in 1962.

A preservation society then bought the line: it was reopened as a tourist attraction in 1968, and has gone from strength to strength ever since. As well as the trains and the stations (which have been restored to represent different historical periods), there is a museum at Ingrow and an exhibition shed at Oxenhope.

Opposite: Opening the level crossing gates at Oakworth, a station restored in Edwardian style

Above: The line has an average 1 in 70 gradient, so the locomotives all face uphill, and have to work hard, as here near Ingrow

Below: At Oxenhope Station

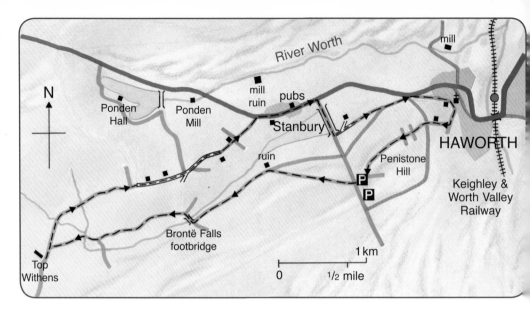

The 'Wuthering Heights' Walk

Distance: 11.8 km (7¼ miles) from the Brontë Parsonage, or 9.3 km (5¾ miles) from the Penistone Hill car park
Time: Allow 3 hours from Penistone Hill, or 3½ from the Parsonage. Please be warned: this is a serious country walk which climbs to an altitude of 425 m (1400 ft) on the Pennine Way. You need to be properly equipped with warm clothes (it will be windy and at least one layer of clothing colder than you expect!) as well as waterproofs and walking boots. The paths are uneven and/or muddy in places. Take a supply of water as well as a compass and map.

From the back of the church, take the PUBLIC FOOTPATH TO PENISTONE HILL AND OXENHOPE, through the graveyard. Turn right into an enclosed footpath leading slightly uphill. After 250 m turn right, TOP WITHENS BRONTE FALLS BRONTE WAY.

Cross a lane and bear left, BRONTE FALLS TOP WITHENS. Ignore cross paths and continue to a track. Turn right into the Penistone Hill car parking area – the alternative starting point.

Cross the road and take the footpath opposite, through a kissing gate and onto the moor. Join a track and pass a ruined farm – the first of many you will see. Follow the main path, which skirts the top edge of a pretty valley, until you reach a little footbridge at what is now called Brontë Falls. Cross the bridge, climb to a kissing gate and turn left, TOP WITHENS.

This path climbs, slowly at first, to a junction with the Pennine Way. Turn left for the last 200 m to the ruined farm. (Another 700 m, and a further 25 m in altitude, would bring you to the Pennine watershed, and into Lancashire.)

Now return to the junction and keep left, STANBURY HAWORTH PENNINE WAY. After 1.4 km, about 150 m before a house, turn very briefly left down a footpath beside a wall until you can see Ponden Reservoir. Almost directly ahead of you, just to the left of the reservoir, is the roof of Ponden Hall, whose site may have inspired Thrushcross Grange in *Wuthering Heights*, though the reservoir is 'new' (1870s).

Now return to the main path, pass the house and fork left, PENNINE WAY STANBURY. Pass Lower Height Farm and at a path crossing continue ahead down the track, HOWARTH STANBURY. The track becomes a lane. Ignore side turnings.

At a T-junction, bear right into Stanbury. Beware of traffic. Walk through the village, passing two pubs, 'The Friendly' and the 'Wuthering Heights', so take your pick! Shortly beyond the village, turn right (OXENHOPE).

At the far side of the reservoir dam, if you started from the Penistone Hill, continue up the road to the car park.

If you started from the church, turn left, BRIDLEWAY TO CEMETERY ROAD. Keep right. Join a lane and continue ahead to a road junction. Walk ahead into Haworth, but after 100 m turn right onto a footpath, which will bring you back to the Parsonage and church.

Top Withens around 1910

Top Withens

In 1872 Ellen Nussey suggested that Top Withens (or Withins) was Emily's inspiration for *Wuthering Heights*. If so, it was only the location, not the building, since that is far smaller than what she describes.

The 1841 Census shows a string of small farms extending out from Stanbury, including three Withens farms. Top Withens, the most distant, was inhabited by Jonas Sunderland (1768-1849) as well as his son, also Jonas (c.1805-1888), his daughter-in-law and his grandson John (1833-1913).

For decades the family continued in occupation of 20 acres, as farmers but also as hand-loom worsted weavers. When John married and started to farm nearby at South Dean, his brother James and later his sister Ann took over Top Withens, though the last mention of hand-loom weaving is in 1861. Ann, by then married to Samuel Sharp, was farming it in 1891, but by 1901 all three Withens were uninhabited.

In 1913, Whiteley Turner said it was empty, but 'a rudely-constructed table and seats, a dinted enamelled kettle, and heaped-up ashes in the grate suggest occasional visits by shepherds.' After the 1914-18 war it seems to have been re-occupied by one Ernest Roddy, who ran it as a poultry farm. (Perhaps he was the Ernest Norman Roddy, born at Ingrow in 1883, called up in 1916, who married in 1924.) In 1926, 'Wuthering Heights' was abandoned for the last time.

Except, of course, that it is *not* Wuthering Heights! That only ever existed in Emily's imagination – and in ours. However fascinating the stone-paved streets and moorland paths trodden by the Brontë sisters, ultimately it is to their novels that we need to return.